Jenni Hicks

FAST&FRESH

FAST&FRESH

quick recipes for busy lives

Louise Pickford

with photography by Peter Cassidy

RYLAND
PETERS
& SMALL
LONDON NEW YORK

Senior Designer Susan Downing
Commissioning Editor Elsa Petersen-Schepelern
Editor Kathy Steer
Production Deborah Wehner
Art Director Gabriella Le Grazie
Publishing Director Alison Starling

Food Stylist Julz Beresford
Prop Stylist Helen Trent
Indexer Hilary Bird

Published in the United Kingdom in 2003
by Ryland Peters & Small
Kirkman House,
12–14 Whitfield Street
London W1T 2RP
www.rylandpeters.com
10 9 8 7 6 5 4 3 2

ISBN 1 84172 403 3

A catalogue record for this book is available from the British Library.

Printed and bound in China.

Notes
All spoon measurements are level.

All eggs are large, unless otherwise specified. Uncooked or partly cooked eggs should
not be served to the very young, the very old, those with compromised immune systems,
or to pregnant women.

Author's acknowledgements
Thank you to everyone at Ryland Peters & Small for their continued support, and also to
my husband, who tastes and assesses everything I cook and still remains impartial.

CONTENTS

FAST FOOD FOR BUSY LIVES

Fast & Fresh is a recipe book for today's cook and will help you to make the best use of time when it comes to preparing a meal. Although in an ideal world it would be nice to saunter at our leisure through food markets or shop at individual suppliers, reality rarely provides us with such luxury. More usual is a quick dash to the supermarket on the way home.

Once in the kitchen, recipes need to be fuss free – no complicated sauces or stocks that take several hours to prepare, but just making the most of good-quality, seasonal produce. I cannot overemphasize the importance of shopping for seasonal produce. Vegetables that were in the ground just a few hours ago would be fantastic, but for most of us this is a bit of a pipe dream. However, buying locally grown produce is both possible and advisable – not only are they likely to taste better than those that have been picked underripe and transported half way round the world, but also they will most likely be far cheaper too.

To me, cooking is more than purely sustenance – it is also a love and passion for creating flavours that delight and dishes that satisfy. It is the pleasure of sitting down with friends and family, sharing thoughts and anecdotes or just enjoying the food and company with a glass of wine. Cooking should be fun not a chore.

Because most of us want a quick fix at the end of a busy day, we often opt for fast or convenience foods that will fill the gap – but do these ever truly satisfy us? What if you could shop, prepare and cook a delicious meal in the time it takes to order and collect that takeaway? With *Fast & Fresh* you can.

Sometimes, especially when I'm in a hurry, I might skip the starter altogether and just concentrate on the main course – and a pudding, of course.

Other times, I make a quick antipasti with my favourite things from the deli counter – perhaps Parma ham, salami and other cold cuts – plus a dish of olives, or toast and dips.

A simple salad also makes a great starter – just crisp green leaves and a vinaigrette, either plain or with blue cheese added. Or something exotic, such as the pea shoots with wasabi-flavoured mayonnaise on page 14. Or use the same wasabi mayonnaise as a dip for some raw fresh vegetables or crudités.

Often however, I think that starters are the most exciting part of a meal. You can turn them into a whole meal if you like – I sometimes make a selection of dishes, so people can dip in, as you do with mezze or tapas. This is a fun way to eat and although you may need a little more time to prepare a selection of dishes, there is little else to do later other than enjoy the meal.

STARTERS

Thai fish, prawn or crab cakes are quick and easy to make —
perfect as a first course, or as a spicy snack with drinks. If you
have time, marinate the prawn mixture for 30 minutes or so.
I keep a few jars of chilli jam on hand, but you can use a
prepared chilli sauce if you prefer.

THAI PRAWN CAKES
WITH CHILLI JAM

To make the chilli jam, put the tomatoes, chillies and garlic into a food processor and
purée until fairly smooth. Transfer to a saucepan, add the ginger, soy sauce, sugar,
vinegar and sea salt, and bring to the boil. Cook for 30–35 minutes, stirring occasionally
until thick and glossy.

Warm the jars in a low oven, pour in the thickened jam and let cool completely. Seal and
store in the refrigerator.

To make the prawn cakes, put the prawns into a food processor and blend to a purée. Add
the lime leaves, spring onions, coriander, egg, fish sauce and rice flour, blend briefly and
transfer to a bowl. Using damp hands, shape the mixture into 24 patties, 5 cm diameter.

Pour 1 cm depth of the oil into a frying pan, heat for 1 minute over medium heat, then
add the cakes, spaced apart. Fry in batches for 2 minutes on each side until golden
brown. Remove and drain on kitchen paper and keep them warm in a low oven while
you cook the remainder. Serve with chilli jam or sweet chilli sauce.

500 g uncooked, shelled prawns

4 lime leaves, very finely chopped

4 spring onions, finely chopped

2 tablespoons chopped fresh coriander

1 egg

1 tablespoon Thai fish sauce

50 g rice flour

peanut or sunflower oil, for frying

chilli jam (below) or
sweet chilli sauce, to serve

chilli jam

500 g ripe tomatoes, coarsely chopped

3–4 red chillies, coarsely chopped

2 garlic cloves, chopped

1 teaspoon grated fresh ginger

2 tablespoons light soy sauce

250 g palm sugar or soft brown sugar

100 ml white wine vinegar

½ teaspoon sea salt

*2 preserving jars, about
200 ml each, sterilized*

serves 6 (makes 24 cakes)

This spicy aubergine dip is like Middle Eastern baba ganoush aubergine purée, with yoghurt instead of tahini. The aubergine should be charred well to achieve the best smoky flavour.

CHAR-GRILLED AUBERGINE DIP

Cut the aubergine lengthways into thin slices, about 2 mm. Put the oil into a small bowl, add the cumin, salt and pepper, mix well, then brush all over the aubergine.

Cook on a preheated stove-top grill pan or under a hot grill for 3–4 minutes on each side until charred and tender. Let cool, then chop finely.

Put the yoghurt into a bowl, then stir in the aubergine, spring onions and lemon juice. Taste and adjust the seasoning with salt and pepper. Serve in bowls or on plates, with toasted pita bread for dipping.

1 large aubergine

2 tablespoons extra virgin olive oil

1 teaspoon ground cumin

200 ml plain yoghurt

2 spring onions, finely chopped

1 tablespoon freshly squeezed lemon juice

sea salt and freshly ground black pepper

toasted pita bread, to serve

serves 6

Tzatziki is widely available and most brands are reliable.This combination can also be made up as a sandwich filling.

SMOKED SALMON BRUSCHETTA
WITH ROCKET AND TZATZIKI

Toast the bread on a preheated stove-top grill pan or under a hot grill. While still hot rub, all over with the garlic and sprinkle with oil. Top each piece with a large spoonful of tzatziki and pile on the salmon and rocket. Season with pepper and serve sprinkled with extra oil.

4 thick slices of sourdough bread

1 large garlic clove, halved

2 tablespoons extra virgin olive oil, plus extra to serve

250 g tzatziki

250 g smoked salmon slices

a handful of rocket

freshly ground black pepper

serves 6

HOMEMADE HERB CHEESE

Put all the ingredients into a bowl and stir well. Line a second bowl with a large piece of muslin and spoon in the yoghurt mixture. Pull up the ends of the muslin to form a bag and tie tightly with string.

Hang the bag over the bowl so the liquid can drain from the yoghurt. Leave in a cool place overnight. Unwrap the bag and transfer the cheese to a serving bowl. Serve with wholemeal or soda bread.

500 g thick yoghurt or 400 g plain yoghurt plus 100 g double cream

1 garlic clove, crushed

3 tablespoons chopped fresh basil

3 tablespoons chopped mixed fresh herbs, including dill, marjoram, parsley and thyme leaves

sea salt and freshly ground black pepper

wholemeal or Soda Bread (page 112)

a piece of muslin, 30 cm square

serves 4–6

Pea shoots are the tendrils and baby leaves of mangetout. You often see them in Chinese and South-east Asian markets, but if you can't find any, use watercress instead. It will give a delicious peppery flavour, which mirrors the fiery spice of wasabi.

PEA SHOOT SALAD
WITH WASABI MAYONNAISE

Heat 5 cm of oil in deep saucepan until it reaches 180°C (350°F) on a sugar thermometer (or a cube of bread crisps and browns in 30 seconds). Break the noodles into 5 cm lengths and add to the oil in 4 batches (be careful because the fat will foam up as the noodles are added). Fry for 1–2 minutes until crisp. Drain on kitchen paper and sprinkle with salt.

Mix the mayonnaise, wasabi and vinegar in a bowl. Add the pea shoots or watercress with the radishes and toss until evenly coated. Top with the noodles and serve at once.

100 g dried Chinese egg noodles, soaked and drained according to the directions on the packet

200 g pea shoots or watercress

125 g radishes, sliced and cut into strips

sea salt

peanut or sunflower oil, for deep-frying

wasabi mayonnaise dressing

1 recipe Mayonnaise (page 142)

1 tablespoon wasabi paste

2 tablespoons rice wine vinegar

serves 4

Yoghurt crusted chicken threaded onto skewers makes ideal finger food for buffets and cocktail parties. The yoghurt tenderizes the chicken and helps the lemon soak into the meat. For the best flavour, cook them on a barbecue – the yoghurt becomes delicious and slightly crunchy.

CHICKEN LEMON SKEWERS

Cut the chicken fillets lengthways into 2 mm thick strips and put into a shallow ceramic dish.

Put all the marinade ingredients into a bowl, stir well and pour over the chicken, turn to coat, cover and let marinate in the refrigerator overnight.

The next day, thread the chicken onto the soaked bamboo skewers, zig-zagging the meat back and forth as you go.

Cook on a preheated barbecue or under a hot grill for 3–4 minutes on each side until charred and tender. Let cool slightly before serving.

500 g skinless chicken breast fillets

marinade

250 ml plain yoghurt

2 tablespoons extra virgin olive oil

2 garlic cloves, crushed

grated zest and freshly squeezed juice of 1 unwaxed lemon

1–2 teaspoons chilli powder

1 tablespoon chopped fresh coriander

sea salt and freshly ground black pepper

12 bamboo skewers, soaked in cold water for 30 minutes

serves 4

VEGETARIAN AND SIDES

This chapter is about cooking vegetables as well as cooking vegetarian food.

Buying seasonal produce will reap great rewards. Though most of us aren't fortunate enough to have a vegetable garden, there are often farmers' or organic markets which offer the best chance of buying ingredients harvested within hours of purchase.

If you have good-quality produce, the rest is easy – add a single herb or spice to compliment a particular vegetable and make a side dish that tastes wonderful and will go well with a whole range of meat and fish.

Living with a non-meat-eater means I eat very little meat myself and, although we both eat fish, vegetable dishes form the basis of our diet. This chapter is great for vegetarians looking for quick and simple recipes, but I hope it will also surprise and inspire many who feel a meat-free meal can be a bit dull.

I often hear it said that vegetarian food is all well and good if you have plenty of time, but that's no help if you're in hurry. Let me dispel that myth and prove it is just as quick and easy to make a meat-free meal as any other.

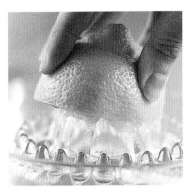

Tabbouleh, the fresh parsley salad from Lebanon, is based on bulghur wheat. This one is made with couscous, the fine Moroccan pasta, now available in an instant version – you just soak it in water or stock for 10 minutes or so.

FRAGRANT HERB COUSCOUS SALAD

To make the fragrant garlic oil, peel the cloves and put them into a saucepan. Add the bay leaves and oil and heat gently for 15 minutes until the garlic has softened. Don't let the garlic brown. Let cool, remove and mash the garlic cloves, then return them to the oil. Refrigerate until required. Use 150 ml for this recipe and reserve the remainder.

Put the couscous into a bowl, add water to cover by 5 cm and let soak for 10 minutes.

Drain the soaked couscous, shaking the sieve well to remove any excess water. Transfer to a bowl, add the fragrant garlic oil, lemon juice, chopped basil, coriander, mint and parsley. Season with salt and pepper, then set aside to develop the flavours until ready to serve. Serve with halved lemons, if using.

300 g instant couscous

freshly squeezed juice of 1 lemon

2 tablespoons chopped fresh basil

2 tablespoons chopped fresh coriander

2 tablespoons chopped fresh mint

2 tablespoons chopped fresh parsley

sea salt and freshly ground black pepper

2 lemons, halved, to serve (optional)

fragrant garlic oil

1 whole head of garlic, cloves separated

2 bay leaves

600 ml extra virgin olive oil

serves 4

1 tablespoon sesame oil

1 onion, sliced

200 g green beans, cut into 5 cm lengths

350 g deep-fried tofu, sliced

2 tablespoons sweet chilli sauce

a handful basil leaves, preferably Thai

2 tablespoons sesame seeds, toasted in
a dry frying pan

sauce

400 ml coconut milk

300 ml Vegetable Stock (page 143)

2 stalks lemongrass, sliced crossways

1 tablespoon Thai fish sauce

8 lime leaves, sliced

2 garlic cloves, chopped

3 cm fresh ginger, peeled and grated

serves 4

Deep-fried tofu cakes are available from Asian shops or health food stores where they can be found in the refrigerator. You can substitute ordinary firm tofu, cut into cubes instead.

STIR-FRIED TOFU
WITH CHILLI COCONUT SAUCE

Put all the sauce ingredients into a saucepan, bring to the boil and simmer for 20 minutes until reduced by half. Strain the sauce and reserve.

Heat the oil in a wok or frying pan and stir-fry the onions and beans for 1 minute, add the tofu cakes and stir-fry for a further 1 minute. Add the coconut sauce, sweet chilli sauce and basil leaves and heat through. Serve sprinkled with the sesame seeds.

PEA AND MINT SOUP

Melt the butter in a saucepan, add the leeks, potatoes and garlic and fry for 10 minutes. Add the peas, stock, mint sprigs and a little salt and pepper and bring to the boil. Cover and simmer for 20 minutes. Discard the mint sprigs.

Transfer the soup to a blender, add the chopped mint, then purée until very smooth. Return to the pan, season to taste and heat through. Serve the soup topped with a spoonful of crème fraîche and a generous grinding of black pepper.

50 g butter

2 leeks, trimmed, split, well washed, then chopped

200 g baking potatoes, chopped

1 garlic clove, crushed

750 g frozen peas

1 litre Chicken or Vegetable Stock (page 143)

2 sprigs of mint

2 tablespoons chopped fresh mint

sea salt and freshly ground black pepper

crème fraîche, to serve

serves 6

We're into fast cooking, so this is a cheat's curry because I have used a ready-made curry paste. Serve with boiled basmati rice.

QUICK VEGETABLE CURRY

Heat the oil in a saucepan and fry the onion, garlic, ginger, curry paste and cinnamon for 5 minutes. Add the potatoes, tomatoes, stock, tomato purée, salt and pepper. Bring to the boil, cover and simmer gently for 20 minutes.

Add the mushrooms, peas, ground almonds and coriander to the pan and cook for a further 10 minutes. Taste and adjust the seasoning with salt and pepper, then serve with basmati rice.

3 tablespoons peanut or sunflower oil

1 onion, sliced

2 garlic cloves, chopped

3 cm fresh ginger, peeled and grated

1 tablespoon hot curry paste

1 teaspoon ground cinnamon

500 g potatoes, cut into cubes

400 g canned chopped tomatoes

300 ml Vegetable Stock (page 143)

1 tablespoon tomato purée

200 g button mushrooms, halved

200 g frozen peas

25 g ground almonds

2 tablespoons chopped fresh coriander

sea salt and freshly ground black pepper

serves 4

2 tablespoons peanut oil

1 tablespoon toasted sesame oil

2 garlic cloves, sliced

1 red chilli, deseeded and sliced

1 kg Savoy cabbage, finely shredded

1 tablespoon chopped fresh coriander

freshly squeezed juice of ½ lemon

50 g dry roasted peanuts

2 tablespoons sesame seeds, toasted

sea salt and ground Szechuan pepper

serves 4

STIR-FRIED SESAME CABBAGE

Heat the two oils together in a wok or large, deep frying pan, add the garlic and chilli and stir-fry over high heat for 30 seconds.

Add the cabbage and stir-fry for a further 2–3 minutes until golden and the cabbage is starting to soften.

Add the coriander, lemon juice, peanuts, sesame seeds, salt and pepper, stir well and transfer to a warmed dish. Serve at once.

Basil oil is particularly good sprinkled onto this simple pastry, but you can use ordinary olive oil. Preheating the baking sheet will make the base of the tart beautifully crisp.

SIMPLE TOMATO AND OLIVE TART
WITH PARMESAN

To make the basil oil, blanch the leaves very briefly in boiling water, drain and dry thoroughly with kitchen paper. Put into a blender, add the oil and salt and blend until very smooth. Strain the oil through a fine sieve, or one lined with muslin. Keep in the refrigerator but return to room temperature before using.

Preheat the oven to 220°C (425°F) Gas 7 and put a baking sheet on the middle shelf.

Roll out the dough on a lightly floured surface to form a rectangle, 25 x 30 cm. Trim the edges and transfer the dough to a second baking sheet. Using the blade of a sharp knife, gently tap the edges several times (this will help the pastry rise and the edges separate) and prick all over with a fork.

Put the tomatoes, olives, basil oil, salt and pepper into a bowl and mix lightly. Spoon the mixture over the pastry and carefully slide the tart directly onto the preheated baking sheet. Bake for 12–15 minutes until risen and golden.

Remove from the oven and sprinkle with the Parmesan. Cut into 4 and serve hot with a handful of rocket leaves.

350 g ready-made puff pastry, thawed if frozen

125 g red cherry tomatoes, halved

125 g yellow cherry tomatoes, halved

50 g semi-dried or sun-dried tomatoes, halved

50 g pitted black olives, halved

2 tablespoons basil oil (below)

25 g freshly grated Parmesan cheese

sea salt and freshly ground black pepper

a handful of rocket leaves, to serve

basil oil

25 g fresh basil leaves

150 ml extra virgin olive oil

a pinch of sea salt

2 baking sheets

serves 4

Red lentils are widely used in Indian cooking to make dhaal – a sauce to serve with rice. They are healthy, nutritious and delicious. Serve this dish as part of an Indian meal.

CURRIED RED LENTILS

Put the onion, garlic and ginger into a food processor and blend to form a fairly smooth purée. Heat the butter in a saucepan, add the purée, tomatoes and spices and fry gently for about 5 minutes.

Add the lentils, stock, lemon juice, salt and pepper, bring to the boil, cover and simmer over low heat for about 20 minutes until the lentils have thickened.

Taste and adjust the seasoning with salt and pepper, then serve topped with a few fried curry leaves, if using.

1 onion, chopped

2 garlic cloves, chopped

3 cm fresh ginger, peeled and grated

40 g butter

350 g tomatoes, chopped

1 tablespoon curry powder

1 teaspoon ground turmeric

½ teaspoon ground cinnamon

350 g red lentils

900 ml Vegetable Stock (page 143)

freshly squeezed juice of ½ lemon

sea salt and freshly ground black pepper

2–3 sprigs of fresh or frozen curry leaves, fried for a few seconds in 2 tablespoons butter (optional)

serves 6

Although it may sound unusual, chocolate is the secret ingredient of this Mexican-inspired dish. It adds a wonderfully rich, intense flavour to the vegetables. Serve with boiled rice, or the Chilli Cornbread on page 115.

QUICK VEGETARIAN MOLE

Heat the oil in a saucepan and fry the onion, pepper, garlic and spices for 5 minutes. Add the sweet potatoes, canned tomatoes, beans, chilli sauce and 300 ml water and bring to the boil. Cover and simmer over gentle heat for 30 minutes.

Stir in the chocolate and fresh coriander and cook for a final 5 minutes. Taste and adjust the seasoning with salt and pepper, then serve.

2 tablespoons peanut or sunflower oil

1 red onion, chopped

1 large red pepper, deseeded and chopped

2 garlic cloves

2 teaspoons ground coriander

1 teaspoon ground cumin

1/2 teaspoon ground cinnamon

400 g sweet potatoes, cut into cubes

400 g canned chopped tomatoes

400 g canned red kidney beans, rinsed and drained

1–2 teaspoons chilli sauce

15–25 g dark chocolate, grated

2 tablespoons chopped fresh coriander

sea salt and freshly ground black pepper

serves 4

---

1 kg mixed baby vegetables, trimmed, washed and peeled as necessary

black bean dressing

2 tablespoons canned black beans, drained, rinsed and drained again

1 garlic clove, crushed

1 teaspoon grated root ginger

1 tablespoon rice wine vinegar

1 tablespoon light soy sauce

100 ml peanut oil

serves 6

STEAMED BABY VEGETABLES
WITH BLACK BEAN DRESSING

To make the dressing, put the beans into a bowl, add 3 tablespoons cold water, mash lightly with a fork, then stir in the garlic, ginger, vinegar, soy sauce and peanut oil.

Steam the vegetables over a saucepan of simmering water, starting with the largest and adding the rest depending on size, until the vegetables are tender. Transfer to a large bowl and pass the dressing around in a separate bowl so guests can help themselves.

This recipe is based on a favourite Greek dish – *gigantes* or 'big beans'. The Quick Tomato Sauce can be made ahead.

2 tablespoons extra virgin olive oil

1 onion, chopped

½ teaspoon dried chilli flakes

800 g canned butter beans, rinsed and drained

1 recipe Quick Tomato Sauce (page 142)

sea salt and freshly ground black pepper

to serve

toast

freshly grated Parmesan cheese

serves 4

BUTTER BEANS
WITH QUICK TOMATO SAUCE

Heat the oil in a saucepan and gently fry the onion and chilli flakes for 10 minutes until softened but not golden.

Add the beans, stir once and then add the quick tomato sauce, bring to the boil, cover with a lid and simmer gently for about 20 minutes. Taste and adjust the seasoning with salt and pepper and serve piled onto toast with a sprinkling of freshly grated Parmesan.

WHITE BEAN SOUP
WITH OLIVE GREMOLATA

Heat the oil in a saucepan and fry the onion, garlic and sage for 5 minutes until golden. Add the potatoes and beans, stir well, then add the stock, bay leaves, salt and pepper.

Bring to the boil, cover and simmer gently for 20 minutes until the potatoes are tender. Transfer half the soup to a blender and blend until smooth. Return to the pan, adjust the seasoning and heat through.

Meanwhile, to make the gremolata, finely chop the olives and mix with lemon zest and parsley. Serve the soup in warm bowls topped with the gremolata.

4 tablespoons extra virgin olive oil

1 large onion, chopped

2 garlic cloves, crushed

1 tablespoon chopped fresh sage

500 g baking potatoes, cut into cubes

800 g canned white beans, drained

1 litre Vegetable Stock (page 143)

2 bay leaves

175 g pitted black olives

grated zest of 1 unwaxed lemon

2 tablespoons chopped fresh parsley

sea salt and freshly ground black pepper

serves 6

EGGSANDCHEESE

Eggs and dairy products are the victims of a bad press and constantly changing reputations. One minute they're bad for people watching their weight – the next, they're good.

A balanced diet is vital for a healthy body, and eggs and dairy products are excellent sources of protein and calcium, which help build strong bones in the young and reduce the chances of osteoporosis in later life. They taste good and are good for you – especially for people who don't eat meat.

The other great thing about egg and cheese dishes is they are usually very quick to make. Take an omelette or scrambled eggs, for instance – ready in minutes. Cheese on toast? A perfect late-night instant snack. I love dishes like these. I find them comforting and familiar, perhaps because they remind me of the food my mother used to cook for me when I was a kid.

Smoked salmon and baked eggs make the perfect breakfast treat – and take no time at all. In fact, if you're having people over at the weekend for brunch, there can be no quicker, easier or more elegant dish to serve as part of the spread.

BAKED EGGS
WITH SMOKED SALMON AND CHIVES

Divide the smoked salmon and chives between the 4 buttered ramekins. Make a small indent in the salmon with the back of a spoon and break an egg into the hollow, sprinkle with a little pepper and spoon the cream over the top.

Put the ramekins into a roasting tin and half-fill the tin with boiling water. Bake in a preheated oven at 180°C (350°F) Gas 4 for 10–15 minutes until the eggs have just set. Remove from the oven, let cool for a few minutes, then serve with toast.

200 g smoked salmon slices, chopped

1 tablespoon chopped fresh chives

4 eggs

4 tablespoons double cream

sea salt and freshly ground black pepper

toast, to serve

4 ramekins, 200 ml each, well buttered

serves 4

This recipe serves two because it's not easy to cook more than this quantity at once. Regular or portobello mushrooms are fine, but if you can find wild mushrooms such as girolle or chanterelle, then you are in for a real treat.

SCRAMBLED EGGS
WITH MUSHROOMS

Wipe the mushrooms with a damp cloth and cut into thick slices. Put the eggs into a bowl, add salt and pepper and whisk until blended.

Melt 40 g of the butter in a large frying pan. As soon as it stops foaming, add the mushrooms, thyme, salt and pepper. Fry over medium heat until lightly browned and the juices are starting to run.

Push the mushrooms to one side of the pan, add the remaining butter, then pour in the beaten eggs, stirring with a fork until almost set.

Gradually stir in the mushrooms from the sides of the pan, cook a moment longer and spoon onto toast. Sprinkle with chopped parsley, if using, and serve with toast.

250 g portobello mushrooms, or mixed wild mushrooms

6 eggs

50 g unsalted butter

2 teaspoons chopped fresh thyme leaves

sea salt and freshly ground black pepper

to serve

chopped fresh parsley (optional)

toast

sautéed mushrooms (optional)

serves 2

Perfectly set eggs spiked with the fragrance of mixed fresh herbs makes a perfect supper dish and I love to dot the frittata with a little ricotta just before the top is grilled. Cut into small squares, frittata makes great finger food.

FRITTATA
WITH FRESH HERBS AND RICOTTA

Put the eggs into a bowl, add the herbs, celery salt, if using, and a good sprinkling of salt and pepper. Beat with a fork.

Preheat the grill. Heat the oil in a non-stick frying pan until hot, then add the egg mixture. Fry over medium heat for 5–6 minutes until almost set. Dot the ricotta over the top and cook under a hot grill until the surface is set and browned.

Let cool slightly, then cut into wedges and serve warm.

6 eggs

a large handful of chopped mixed fresh herbs, such as basil, chervil, chives, marjoram, mint and/or parsley

1 teaspoon celery salt (optional)

2 tablespoons extra virgin olive oil

125 g fresh ricotta cheese, crumbled into big pieces

sea salt and freshly ground black pepper

serves 4

BAKED CHEVRE

Put the chèvre slices onto the prepared baking sheet, sprinkle with a little oil, dot with thyme leaves and season with pepper. Bake in a preheated oven at 200°C (400°F) Gas 6 for 10–12 minutes until just starting to ooze and run.

Meanwhile, toast the sourdough and rub it with the garlic. When the cheese is ready, spread it onto the toasted, garlicky sourdough and serve with a green salad.

4 thick slices of chèvre cheese with rind, 50 g per serving

extra virgin olive oil, for sprinkling

1 tablespoon chopped fresh thyme

freshly ground black pepper

to serve

4 slices of sourdough bread

1–2 garlic cloves, halved

green salad

a baking sheet, lined with foil

serves 4

Simple and delicious, this recipe can be served as a starter or as a snack with a green salad. Use a creamy goats' cheese with a rind that will soften nicely without melting.

GRILLED ASPARAGUS
WITH GOATS' CHEESE AND HERB OIL

Trim the asparagus spears and rub or brush with a little of the Thyme Oil, scatter with salt and pepper and cook under a hot grill for 4–5 minutes, turning half-way through until charred and tender.

Arrange on plates and top each one with a slice of the cheese, return to the grill very briefly until the cheese is softened but not browned. Sprinkle with more Thyme Oil and serve with crusty bread.

500 g asparagus spears

1 tablespoon Thyme Oil (page 140), plus extra to serve

125 g goats' cheese, sliced

sea salt and freshly ground black pepper

baguette, to serve

serves 4

This is one of those dishes I crave when I get back late from the cinema or a show – quick, delicious and washing-up-free. It tastes great with almost any chutney or relish. Be ready to provide seconds.

CHEESE ON TOAST

Toast the bread under the grill on one side only. Grate the cheese onto the untoasted side of the bread (if using very soft cheese, slice it instead). Add a few drops of Worcestershire sauce, if using, and grill for 2–3 minutes until melted and bubbling.

Serve on a platter with the bottle of pickles, relish or chutney and a spoon so that guests can help themselves.

2 thick slices of white bread

125 g cheese, such as Cheddar, a soft creamy goats' cheese or Brie

a few drops of Worcestershire sauce (optional)

pickles, relish or chutney, to serve

serves 2

Make this dish only when top-quality fresh figs are in season. Otherwise use peaches, nectarines or melon wedges.

FIGS WITH MARINATED FETA

Put the garlic, chile, lemon zest, cumin, mint, and oil into a bowl, add the feta and toss gently. Set aside to marinate for at least 30 minutes (this can be done the night before).

Slice the figs in half and serve on the toasted bread with the feta and marinade juices, then serve sprinkled with a little Reduced Balsamic Vinegar.

1 garlic clove, crushed

1 red chilli, deseeded and chopped

grated zest of 1 unwaxed lemon

$1/2$ teaspoon ground cumin

1 tablespoon chopped fresh mint

6 tablespoons extra virgin olive oil

250 g feta cheese, chopped

4–6 large ripe figs

4 slices toasted sourdough bread

cracked black pepper

Reduced Balsamic Vinegar, to serve (page 141)

serves 4

Served warm, these soufflés are a favourite of mine because I don't have to panic getting them to the table before they sink! Make sure you butter the ramekin dishes very well so that you can get the soufflés out.

WARM GOATS' CHEESE SOUFFLES

Melt the butter in a saucepan, add the flour and cook over low heat for 30 seconds. Remove the pan from the heat and gradually stir in the milk until smooth. Return to the heat and stir constantly until the mixture thickens. Cook for 1 minute.

Cool slightly and beat in the cheese, egg yolks, herbs, salt and pepper. Put the egg whites into a bowl and whisk until soft peaks form. Fold the egg whites into the cheese mixture.

Spoon the mixture into the ramekins and bake in a preheated oven 200°C (400°F) Gas 6 for 15–18 minutes until risen and golden on top. Remove from the oven and let cool for about 15 minutes.

Using a palette knife, work round the edges of the soufflés and turn them out onto plates. Serve with rocket salad.

25 g unsalted butter

2 tablespoons plain flour

250 ml milk

100 g soft goats' cheese

3 eggs, separated

2 tablespoons chopped fresh mixed herbs, such as basil, chives, mint and tarragon

sea salt and freshly ground black pepper

rocket salad, to serve

6 ramekins, 200 ml each, well buttered

serves 6

FISHANDSEAFOOD

Since moving to Australia, I have learned a great deal about the freshness of seafood, something that is unfortunately not always available in other countries.

However, top-quality seafood can be found, and it is usually just a case of seeking out a good supplier. Supermarkets are improving all the time and will only continue to do so if you, the customer, demand quality.

Don't be afraid to talk to your fishmongers, ask them questions – most are only too glad to share their knowledge.

When shopping for shellfish, avoid any that are sitting in water, and when buying fish, look for bright eyes and shiny skin. They should smell of the sea (not at all fishy).

Simplicity is the name of the game when you're cooking seafood. Let the flavours speak for themselves by serving it quickly cooked and simply dressed – perhaps just with a sprinkle of oil and fragrant chopped herbs or a pat of spiced butter.

Prawns make the fastest, freshest most impressive dish you can imagine. If you can't find uncooked prawns, use precooked ones – just sprinkle them with the chilli oil and lemon juice and serve with the cool and refreshing pesto. Now, how complicated can that be!

PRAWNS WITH CHILLI OIL
AND PISTACHIO AND MINT PESTO

To make the pesto, put the nuts, mint, garlic and spring onions into a food processor and grind coarsely. Add the oil and purée until fairly smooth and green. Stir in the vinegar and season to taste. Set aside while you prepare the prawns, or store in the refrigerator for up to 5 days.

Put the prawns into a shallow dish and sprinkle with the Chilli Oil, salt and pepper. Cover and let marinate for at least 30 minutes or longer, if possible.

When ready to serve, thread the prawns onto skewers and cook on a preheated barbecue or stove-top grill pan, or under a hot grill, for about 2 minutes on each side until charred and tender – the flesh should be just opaque. Do not overcook or the prawns will be tough.

Serve on separate plates or a large platter, sprinkle with fresh lemon juice and serve with the pesto and crusty bread to mop up the juices.

24 large uncooked prawns, shelled and deveined

4 tablespoons Chilli Oil (page 140)

freshly squeezed juice of 1 lemon

pistachio and mint pesto

50 g shelled pistachio nuts

a bunch of fresh mint

1 garlic clove, crushed

2 spring onions, chopped

125 ml extra virgin olive oil

1 tablespoon white wine vinegar

sea salt and freshly ground black pepper

to serve

1 lemon, cut into wedges

crusty bread

serves 4

Try to find the small vongole clams, which tend to be sweeter and more tender than the larger varieties. This recipe will serve four as a starter, but you can serve it with other Asian dishes plus rice and noodles for an impressive banquet.

DRUNKEN CLAMS

Tap each clam lightly on the work surface and discard any that won't close. Put the clams into a saucepan, add the stock, rice wine, garlic, ginger, spring onions and chilli. Grind Szechuan pepper over the top and bring to the boil. Cover with a lid and let steam for 3–4 minutes until all the shells have opened.

Discard any unopened clams and transfer the rest to warmed bowls. Strain the stock through a fine sieve, pour over the clams, then serve.

2 kg fresh clams, well scrubbed

150 ml Fish or Vegetable Stock (page 143)

100 ml Shaohsing (sweetened Chinese rice wine) or sweet sherry

4 garlic cloves, sliced

3 cm fresh ginger, peeled and sliced

6 spring onions, sliced

1 red chilli, deseeded and sliced

Szechuan pepper or black pepper

serves 4

A simple dish with lovely flavours – when you serve lobster, the effect is instantly luxurious and 'special occasion'. Who would ever know this dish was so simple to prepare? Slice the fennel as finely as possible, using a mandoline if you have one. If not, it's worthwhile investing in one so you can cut vegetables very finely – into slices or matchsticks. Inexpensive, but effective, plastic Japanese mandolines are available from kitchen shops.

LOBSTER AND FENNEL SALAD

Trim off and discard the tough outer layer of fennel, then chop and reserve the fronds. Cut the bulb in half, then cut crossways into very thin slices. Put into a bowl, add the lemon juice, oil, fennel fronds, salt and pepper, toss well, then marinate for 15 minutes.

Cut the lobsters in half and lift the tail flesh out of the shell. Crack the claws with a small hammer or crab crackers and carefully remove all the meat.

Put a layer of shaved fennel salad on each plate, top with the lobster and serve with a spoonful of mayonnaise.

1 large bulb of fennel

freshly squeezed juice of ½ lemon

4 tablespoons extra virgin olive oil

4 small cooked lobsters, about 500 g each, or 2 large ones

1 recipe Mayonnaise (page 142)

sea salt and freshly ground black pepper

serves 4

The squid will curl up as they cook, so I use a pair of tongs to open them out again and press flat. You could also put a heatproof plate on top to keep them that way. Take care not to overcook squid or it will be tough.

SEARED SQUID
WITH LEMON AND CORIANDER DRESSING

To make the dressing, put the ingredients into a screw-top jar, shake until amalgamated and use as required. If storing in the refrigerator, omit the coriander and add it just before use.

Cut the squid bodies in half and open out flat. Brush with the olive oil and season with salt and pepper.

Heat a stove-top grill pan for 5 minutes until very hot. Add the squid bodies and tentacles and cook for 1 minute on each side until charred and tender. Transfer to a board and cut the squid into thick slices.

Put the dressing into a bowl, add the squid and toss well. Serve with a few baby spinach leaves and extra black pepper.

Note Squid is very easy to clean. Pull out the tentacles (the insides should come with them). Cut off the tentacles and discard the insides. Rinse out the bodies, pulling out the stiff transparent quill, like a little wand of plastic. That's it.

4 medium squid, cleaned, about 750 g

1 tablespoon extra virgin olive oil

sea salt and freshly ground black pepper

baby spinach leaves, to serve

lemon and coriander dressing

5 tablespoons peanut oil

1 tablespoon toasted sesame oil

freshly squeezed juice of 1 lemon

2 tablespoons sweet soy sauce, (Indonesian *ketchap manis*, or regular soy sauce with $1/2$ teaspoon sugar)

2 tablespoons chopped fresh coriander

1 garlic clove, crushed

serves 4

Scallops, with their sweet flesh and subtle hint of the sea, are a real treat. Truffle oil, though expensive, is used sparingly and transforms this dish into something special. If you don't have any truffle oil, use either Thyme Oil (page 140) or Fragrant Garlic Oil (page 21).

SEARED SCALLOPS
WITH CRUSHED POTATOES

Cook the potatoes in a saucepan of lightly salted, boiling water until just tender. Drain well and return to the pan. Lightly crush them with a fork leaving them still a little chunky. Add the olive oil, olives, parsley and a few drops of truffle oil, if using. Season with salt and pepper and stir well.

Put the scallops into a bowl, add the olive oil, salt and pepper. Sear the scallops on a preheated stove-top grill pan for 1 minute on each side (don't overcook or they will be tough). Remove to a plate and let them rest briefly.

Put a pile of crushed potatoes onto each plate, put the scallops on top and sprinkle with a few extra drops of truffle oil, if using.

12 large scallops, corals removed

1 tablespoon extra virgin olive oil

sea salt and freshly ground black pepper

crushed potatoes

500 g new potatoes, peeled

1 tablespoon extra virgin olive oil

25 g pitted black olives, chopped

1 tablespoon chopped
fresh flat leaf parsley

a few drops of truffle oil (optional)

sea salt and freshly ground black pepper

serves 4

Peppery radish and fresh mint yoghurt tempers the heat from the spice-coated fish, though if you don't like very spicy food, you could leave out the chilli powder and rely on the freshly ground black pepper and crunchy radishes alone. Serve crusty bread on the side to mop up the juices.

BLACKENED MONKFISH
WITH RADISH AND MINT YOGHURT

Mix all the spice ingredients together and sprinkle on a plate. Roll the fish in the spice mix until well coated.

Melt the butter and oil in a frying pan, then as soon as it stops foaming add the fish. Fry over medium heat for 8 minutes until browned all over. Transfer to a warm oven and let rest for 5 minutes.

Put the yoghurt into a bowl, add the radishes, cucumber, mint, garlic, salt and pepper and stir well. Serve with the browned fish.

4 fillets monkfish or cod, 200 g each, skinned if necessary

50 g unsalted butter

1 tablespoon peanut oil

200 g plain yoghurt

4 radishes, cut into matchsticks, plus extra to serve

1/2 cucumber, peeled, deseeded and cut into matchsticks

1 tablespoon chopped fresh mint

1 garlic clove, crushed

sea salt and freshly ground black pepper

spice mix

2 tablespoons chopped fresh thyme leaves

1 tablespoon ground cumin

1 tablespoon salt

2 teaspoons ground allspice

2 teaspoons crushed black pepper

1/2 teaspoon chilli powder

serves 4

Salmon is always better a little pink in the middle. If you cook fish too long, it will become dry and tasteless. To avoid this, sear it on the skin side first at a fairly high heat. The skin will caramelize a little, then when you turn it over you need only brown the flesh side for a short time. Very fast and fresh!

SEARED SALMON

WITH CUCUMBER PICKLE

To make the cucumber pickle, cut the cucumber in half lengthways, scoop out and discard the seeds and cut the flesh into 1 cm slices. Put the salt, rice vinegar, sugar, chilli and ginger into a bowl, add 4 tablespoons water and mix well. Pour over the cucumber and set aside to marinate.

Brush the salmon fillets with the sesame oil and season with salt and crushed Szechuan pepper. Put the fillets skin side down onto a preheated stove-top grill pan and cook for 4 minutes. Turn the salmon and cook for a further 1 minute.

Remove from the pan, let rest for a few moments, then serve with the cucumber pickle and a crisp green salad.

4 salmon fillets, 200 g each

1 tablespoon sesame oil

salt and crushed Szechuan pepper or black pepper

green salad, to serve

cucumber pickle

1 cucumber, about 20 cm long

2 teaspoons salt

4 tablespoons rice vinegar

3 tablespoons caster sugar

1 red chilli, deseeded and sliced

3 cm fresh ginger, peeled and grated

serves 4

I love to serve this dish whenever I see some really fresh swordfish at the market. It is easy to overcook swordfish, which will become tough, so follow the timings below and err on the side of caution – you can always put the fish back on the heat for a moment or two longer if necessary.

SEARED SWORDFISH
WITH NEW POTATOES, BEANS AND OLIVES

Brush the swordfish steaks with 1 tablespoon of the oil, season with salt and pepper and set aside.

To make the dressing, put the remaining oil into a bowl, add the lemon juice, sugar, chives and salt and pepper, beat well and set aside.

Cook the potatoes in a saucepan of lightly salted boiling water for 10 minutes, add the beans and cook for a further 3–4 minutes or until the potatoes and beans are just tender. Drain well, add the olives and half the dressing and toss well.

Cook the swordfish steaks on a preheated barbecue or stove-top grill pan for about 1½ minutes on each side. Let rest in a warm oven for 5 minutes, then serve with the warm potato salad, sprinkled with the remaining dressing and the balsamic vinegar.

4 swordfish steaks, 200 g each

7 tablespoons extra virgin olive oil

2 tablespoons lemon juice

½ teaspoon caster sugar

1 tablespoon chopped fresh chives

500 g new potatoes, halved if large

200 g green beans, trimmed

50 g pitted black olives, chopped

sea salt and freshly ground black pepper

Reduced Balsamic Vinegar (page 141),
to serve

serves 4

POULTRY AND MEAT

I grew up on a farm where we kept hens that were allowed to feed on the grain left behind after the corn had been harvested. These birds gorged themselves happily on such wonderful food that the benefits to both them and us were obvious for anyone lucky enough to taste them. Now I always buy organic, free-range chicken. It is more expensive, but worth every penny.

For many people, duck is probably seen as a bit of a luxury, because it is expensive and is sometimes difficult to find. However, it is ideal for cooks short of time, because the breasts cook very quickly. They are sold in many supermarkets, or you can buy a whole duck from the butchers and ask them to cut it into joints for you (freeze the rest for another time).

When shopping for meat, look for flesh with a good deep colour and a layer of fat around it which will keep it moist during cooking. Fat should be creamy in colour and almost matt in appearance.

Remember, whatever meat you are cooking, it will need a little time to rest before eating, this lets the meat relax so it is more tender.

Jerk seasoning is Jamaica's popular spice mix, used to spark up meat, poultry and fish, especially the delicious barbecued offerings sold at the roadside jerk huts so beloved of tourists and locals alike. The seasoning is a combination of allspice, cinnamon, chilli, nutmeg, thyme and sugar and is widely available in powder or paste form from larger supermarkets and specialist food stores.*

JERK CHICKEN WINGS
WITH AVOCADO SALSA

Put the chicken wings in a ceramic dish. Mix the oil, jerk seasoning, lemon juice and salt in a bowl, pour over the wings and stir well until evenly coated. Let marinate overnight in the refrigerator.

The next day cook the wings either on a barbecue or under a hot grill for 5–6 minutes each side, basting occasionally with any remaining marinade until charred and tender.

Meanwhile, to make the salsa, put all the ingredients into a bowl, mix well and season to taste. Serve the wings with the salsa.

*Note If you don't have any jerk seasoning on hand, try another spice mix or spice paste instead. Just remember, jerk is very fiery indeed, so you need a spicy one.

12 chicken wings

2 tablespoons extra virgin olive oil

1 tablespoon jerk seasoning powder or 2 tablespoons paste

freshly squeezed juice of ½ lemon

1 teaspoon salt

avocado salsa

1 large ripe avocado

2 ripe tomatoes, peeled, deseeded and chopped

1 garlic clove, crushed

1 small red chilli, deseeded and chopped

freshly squeezed juice of ½ lemon

2 tablespoons chopped fresh coriander

1 tablespoon extra virgin olive oil

sea salt and freshly ground black pepper

serves 4

Chinese five-spice powder is a ready-made spice mix used widely in Asian cooking. It is made up of cassia bark (similar to cinnamon), cloves, fennel, star anise and Szechuan pepper.

ROAST FIVE-SPICE CHICKEN
WITH GINGER BOK CHOY

Wash and dry the chicken pieces and put into a roasting tin.

Put the oil, five-spice powder, ginger and salt into a bowl, mix well, then brush all over the chicken. Roast in a preheated oven at 200°C (400°F) Gas 6 for 25 minutes.

Put the honey and soy sauce into a small saucepan and heat until the honey has melted. Stir well, then brush all over the chicken to form a glaze. Return to the oven and roast for a further 10 minutes until the skin is crisp and golden.

To prepare the bok choy, put the soy sauce, chilli sauce and 4 tablespoons water into a bowl and mix well.

Heat the two oils in a wok or large frying pan, add the ginger and stir-fry for 30 seconds. Add the bok choy and continue to stir-fry for a further 2 minutes. Add the soy sauce mixture, cover and simmer gently for 2 minutes, then serve with the chicken.

4 chicken quarters (breasts or legs)

2 tablespoons sunflower oil

1 teaspoon Chinese five-spice powder

3 cm fresh ginger, peeled and grated

½ teaspoon salt

3 tablespoons honey

1½ tablespoons dark soy sauce

ginger bok choy

3 tablespoons dark soy sauce

1 tablespoon sweet chilli sauce

2 tablespoons sunflower oil

2 teaspoons toasted sesame oil

3 cm fresh ginger, peeled and finely sliced into matchstick strips

8 small bok choy, halved, well washed and patted dry with kitchen paper

serves 4

A great supper dish – simple and quick. Serve it with a green salad, or with this more substantial dish of beans and leeks, which is also very good with lamb. The Mustard and Tarragon Butter is versatile and also tastes wonderful with fish such as salmon.

PAN-FRIED CHICKEN
WITH CREAMY BEANS AND LEEKS

To cook the beans and leeks, melt the butter in a saucepan, add the leeks, garlic and rosemary and fry gently for 5 minutes until softened but not golden.

Add the beans, stir once, then pour in the stock. Bring to the boil, cover and simmer for 15 minutes. Remove the lid, stir in the cream, add salt and pepper to taste, then simmer, uncovered, for a further 5 minutes until the sauce has thickened. Set aside while you prepare the chicken.

Season the chicken with salt and pepper. Heat the butter and oil in a frying pan and as soon as the butter stops foaming cook the chicken skin side down for 4 minutes, turn it over and cook for a further 4 minutes.

Top each breast with a couple of slices of the Mustard and Tarragon Butter and let rest for 2–3 minutes in a warm oven. Serve with the beans and a simple watercress salad.

4 boneless chicken breasts

25 g butter

1 tablespoon extra virgin olive oil

1 recipe Mustard and Tarragon Butter (page 140)

sea salt and freshly ground black pepper

watercress salad, to serve

creamy flageolet beans with leeks

50 g butter

2 leeks, finely chopped

1 garlic clove, crushed

2 teaspoons chopped fresh rosemary

800 g canned flageolet beans, drained, rinsed and drained again

300 ml Vegetable Stock (page 143)

4 tablespoons double cream

sea salt and freshly ground black pepper

serves 4

These mini chickens can be roasted in about 40 minutes. To make sure they are cooked through, push a skewer into the leg meat right down to the bone – if the juices run clear, the bird is cooked. If not, return to the oven for a little longer.

GARLIC-ROASTED POUSSINS

Boil the garlic cloves in a saucepan of lightly salted water for 15 minutes, drain and pat dry (this can be done ahead of time).

Meanwhile, wash the poussins, pat them dry and rub all over with the cut lemon. Chop the lemon into small chunks and put them and the thyme into the body cavities. Season generously with salt and pepper and rub the birds all over with 40 g of the butter.

Put 1 garlic clove into each bird, then put the rest into a large roasting tin. Sit the poussins on top and roast in a preheated oven at 200°C (400°F) Gas 6 for 40 minutes.

Transfer the poussins and garlic cloves to a large plate, wrap loosely in foil and let rest for 10 minutes.

Meanwhile, to make a gravy, spoon off any excess fat from the roasting tin. Add the wine, bring to the boil and scrape any sediments into the wine. Boil until reduced by two-thirds. Add the stock and boil for 5 minutes, or until reduced by half. Put the remaining butter and the flour into a bowl and beat until smooth. Gradually whisk into the gravy, stirring over gentle heat until thickened.

Serve the poussins with the garlic and gravy.

2 whole heads of garlic, separated

2 large poussins

½ lemon

4 sprigs of thyme

50 g butter, softened

100 ml white wine

300 ml Chicken Stock (page 143)

1 tablespoon plain flour

sea salt and freshly ground black pepper

serves 4

Duck breasts make a quick and easy dish. Cook them in a stove-top grill pan or heavy-based frying pan. The skin will turn very black and crispy from the sugar, and the rich flesh is balanced perfectly by the sweetness of spiced plums.

DUCK WITH SPICED PLUMS

Using a sharp knife, cut several slashes in the duck skin. Rub the skin with salt and pepper. Put the honey and soy sauce into a shallow dish, stir well, add the duck breasts and let marinate for at least 15 minutes.

Put the vinegar, sugar, cinnamon and 2 tablespoons water into a saucepan and heat until the sugar dissolves. Bring to the boil, add the plums and simmer gently for 8–10 minutes until the plums have softened. Let cool.

Meanwhile, heat a stove-top grill pan or heavy-based frying pan until hot, add the duck skin side down and cook over medium heat for 5 minutes. Turn and cook for a further 4–5 minutes, then remove from the heat and let rest in a low oven for 5 minutes.

Slice the duck crossways and serve with the plums and a little of the spiced juice.

4 duck breasts, 200 g each

1 tablespoon honey

1 tablespoon dark soy sauce

25 ml rice wine vinegar

25 g palm sugar or soft brown sugar

1/4 teaspoon ground cinnamon

4 plums, halved and stoned

sea salt and freshly ground black pepper

serves 4

A simple dish – the Japanese ingredients such as pickled ginger and seven-spice are available in any supermarket selling sushi ingredients. However, go sparingly with the seven-spice pepper – it's a hot little number.

JAPANESE BEEF TATAKI

Brush the beef fillet with the oil and dust very lightly with the seven-spice pepper. Heat a heavy-based frying pan for 5 minutes until very hot, then add the beef and sear on all sides for 2–3 minutes until evenly browned. Remove from the pan and let cool.

Put the dipping sauce ingredients into a bowl, add 4 tablespoons water, mix well, then divide between 4 small dipping bowls.

Using a very sharp knife, slice the beef thinly and arrange on plates with a little mound of daikon and ginger on each one. Serve with the dipping sauce.

250 g beef fillet, in a piece

1 tablespoon sunflower oil

Japanese seven-spice pepper (*shichimi togarashi*)

5 cm piece daikon (mooli or white radish), peeled and grated

Japanese pickled ginger

dipping sauce

4 tablespoons Japanese soy sauce

4 teaspoons sake or mirin (sweetened Japanese rice wine)

serves 4

It's important to rest meat for a short time before serving to let it relax and the juices from the steak mingle with the butter. You can serve it with any kind of flavoured butter – make up several different kinds, roll them into logs, wrap them in foil and store them in the freezer to use whenever you need a fast and flavourful addition to a dish. They are good with beef, fish, poultry and even vegetables.

PAN-FRIED FILLET STEAK
WITH HORSERADISH BUTTER

To make the horseradish and chive butter, put the butter, horseradish and chives into a bowl and beat well. Season to taste with salt and pepper. Form into a log, wrap in foil and chill for about 30 minutes.

Season the steaks with salt and pepper. Heat the oil in a frying pan and fry the steaks over medium-high heat for 3 minutes on each side for rare, a little longer for medium.

Top each steak with 2 slices of the horseradish butter and set aside to rest in a warm oven for 5 minutes, then serve with the sautéed potatoes and salad.

4 fillet steaks, about 200 g each

2 tablespoons extra virgin olive oil

sea salt and freshly ground black pepper

horseradish and chive butter

125 g unsalted butter, softened

1½ tablespoons grated fresh horseradish

1 tablespoon chopped fresh chives

to serve (optional)

sautéed potatoes

green salad

serves 4

The spices and flavourings used in this recipe are typical of North African cooking, and all over the region, pita bread is stuffed with grilled meat, salad and yoghurt. Use other minced meats if you prefer.

LAMB IN PITA BREAD

Put the coriander and cumin seeds into a small frying pan without oil and fry until they start to brown and release their aroma. Let cool slightly, then grind to powder in a spice grinder (use a clean coffee grinder) or with a mortar and pestle.

Heat the oil in a frying pan, add the onion, garlic and ground spices and fry gently for 5 minutes until softened but not golden. Increase the heat, add the lamb and the pinch of salt and stir-fry for 5–8 minutes until well browned. Stir in the fresh coriander.

Meanwhile, lightly toast the pita bread and cut a long slit in the side of each one. Carefully fill with a few salad leaves, add the minced lamb mixture, a spoonful of yoghurt or tahini and sprinkle with sesame seeds. Serve hot.

2 teaspoons coriander seeds

1 teaspoon cumin seeds

2 tablespoons extra virgin olive oil

1 onion, finely chopped

2 garlic cloves, crushed

1 teaspoon ground cinnamon

$\frac{1}{4}$–$\frac{1}{2}$ teaspoon cayenne pepper

300 g minced lamb

a pinch of salt

2 tablespoons chopped fresh coriander leaves

4 pita breads

a few salad leaves, such as cos lettuce and watercress

plain yoghurt or tahini sauce

1 tablespoon white sesame seeds, toasted in a dry frying pan

serves 4

Pork can easily become dry. The solution is not to cook it at too high a heat, and in this recipe the sage and Parma ham wrapping help to keep it moist. They have the added advantage of lending more flavour as well. Add the fillets to the pan seam side down so the ham doesn't unwrap during cooking.

PARMA-WRAPPED PORK FILLET
WITH SPINACH AND LENTIL SALAD

Cut the pork fillets in half crossways to make 4 servings. Season with salt and pepper. Put 2 slices of Parma ham on a work surface, overlapping them slightly. Add 3 of the sage leaves in a line down the middle. Top with a pork fillet and roll up, keeping the join underneath. Repeat with the remaining fillets.

Heat half the oil in a frying pan, add the pork fillets seam side down and fry over medium heat for about 12–15 minutes, turning frequently until evenly browned. Transfer to a warm oven and let rest for 5 minutes.

Meanwhile, add the remaining oil to the pan, add the shallots, garlic and the 1 tablespoon chopped sage and fry for 3 minutes until softened but not golden. Add the lentils, chicken stock and lemon juice and heat through for 2–3 minutes. Stir in the spinach, cook until just wilted and serve with the pork.

2 pork fillets, 350 g each

8 thin slices of Parma ham

12 large sage leaves, plus
1 tablespoon chopped fresh sage

3 tablespoons extra virgin olive oil

4 shallots, finely chopped

1 garlic clove, crushed

800 g canned lentils, drained

100 ml Chicken Stock (page 143)

freshly squeezed juice of $\frac{1}{2}$ lemon

125 g baby spinach leaves

sea salt and freshly ground black pepper

serves 4

The credit for this recipe goes to my mother, who recently served leftover fruit compote (the remains of a mad day's jam making) with pork chops. It was delicious. Fry the meat over medium heat so you don't burn the wonderful pan juices, which you then pour over the finished dish.

PORK STEAKS
WITH APPLE AND BLACKBERRY COMPOTE

To make the sauce, put the apples, blackberries, sugar, lemon juice, juniper berries and 2 tablespoons water into a saucepan. Cover and cook gently until the fruits have softened. Remove the lid and simmer until the juices have evaporated. Remove from the heat, but keep the mixture warm.

Season the steaks with salt and pepper. Melt the butter in a large frying pan and, as soon as it stops foaming, add the pork. Cook over medium heat for 3–4 minutes on each side until browned and cooked through.

Let rest in a warm oven for 5 minutes. Meanwhile add the sage leaves to the same pan and fry for a few seconds until crispy. Serve the steaks topped with a spoonful of the compote, the sage leaves and pan juices.

4 large pork steaks, about 250 g each

50 g butter

12 large sage leaves

sea salt and freshly ground black pepper

apple and blackberry compote

250 g cooking apples, cored and cut into thin wedges

75 g blackberries

2 tablespoons sugar

freshly squeezed juice of 1/2 lemon

3 juniper berries

serves 4

Pasta, rice and noodles play a major role in cuisines around the world – from Asia and India to the Mediterranean and the Middle East, and the rest of the world has adopted them with open arms.

There are many different varieties of rice used in these countries, including basmati in India and Pakistan, sticky rice and black rice in South-east Asia, the huge number of different rices in Japan, and of course the short grain Italian rice used in risotto. In most rice-producing countries, rice is served at every meal, much as we serve bread in the West. Well, not always!

Noodles are used throughout Asia much as pasta is served in the Mediterranean, and form the basis of many dishes.

These staples provide our main source of carbohydrate and I love them as much for their versatility as their taste. You could cook pasta, noodle and rice dishes every day of the week without ever feeling bored.

PASTARICENOODLES

Most noodle dishes take just a matter of minutes to cook –
in fact, noodles made of rice flour or mung bean starch are
ready almost instantly. Wheat-based noodles take the most
time – but even then, only about the same as regular pasta.

GINGERED CHICKEN NOODLES

Put the rice wine and cornflour into a bowl and mix well. Cut the chicken into small

chunks, add to the bowl, stir well and set aside to marinate while you prepare the

remaining ingredients.

Soak the noodles according to the instructions on the packet, then drain and shake dry.

Put all the sauce ingredients into a small bowl and mix well.

Heat half the oil in a wok or large frying pan, then add the chicken and stir-fry for

2 minutes until golden. Remove to a plate and wipe the pan clean. Add the remaining oil,

then the ginger and mangetout and fry for 1 minute. Return the chicken to the pan, then

add the noodles and sauce. Heat through for 2 minutes.

Add the garlic chives and cashew nuts, stir well and serve.

2 tablespoons rice wine, such as
Chinese Shaohsing or Japanese mirin

2 teaspoons cornflour

350 g skinless chicken breasts

175 g Chinese dried egg noodles

3 tablespoons peanut or sunflower oil

3 cm fresh ginger, peeled and finely
sliced into shreds

125 g mangetout, finely sliced

4 tablespoons chopped fresh
garlic chives or chives

125 g cashew nuts, toasted in
a dry frying pan, then chopped

sauce

100 ml Chicken Stock (page 143)

2 tablespoons dark soy sauce

1 tablespoon lemon juice

1 tablespoon sesame oil

2 teaspoons soft brown sugar

serves 4

The instant dashi stock and miso soup stock used in Japanese cooking are available from some larger supermarkets or Asian food stores. Alternatively use good-quality fresh fish stock.

UDON NOODLES
WITH SEVEN-SPICE SALMON

To cook the noodles, plunge them into a saucepan of boiling water, return to the boil and simmer for 4 minutes until tender. Drain and refresh under cold water, drain again and pat dry with kitchen paper.

Put the dashi or miso stock into a saucepan, add the mirin, soy sauce, tofu, spring onions and wakame and bring to the boil.

Brush the salmon with the oil and dust with a little seven-spice powder. Put the fillets skin side down on a preheated stove-top grill pan for 4 minutes, then turn and cook for a further 1 minute.

Divide the noodles between 4 deep warmed soup bowls, then add the stock, tofu and vegetables. Put the salmon on top and serve.

250 g udon noodles

1.5 litres dashi or miso stock (see recipe introduction)

50 ml mirin (sweetened Japanese rice wine)

50 ml dark soy sauce

100 g firm tofu, cubed

6 spring onions, trimmed and sliced

a few strands of dried wakame seaweed

4 salmon fillets, 200 g each

1 tablespoon sunflower or peanut oil

Japanese seven-spice pepper (*shichimi togarashi*), (see recipe introduction, page 79)

serves 4

'Tartare' means uncooked and, to serve fish this way, you must use very fresh, sashimi-grade tuna. If you prefer your tuna cooked, sear it on a preheated stove-top grill pan for 1 minute on each side or until cooked to your liking. However, I do urge you to try it tartare – it is delicious, as the Japanese well know.

CHILLI TUNA TARTARE PASTA

Cook the pasta according to the instructions on the packet.

Meanwhile, heat the oil in a frying pan, add the garlic and fry gently for 2 minutes until lightly golden. Add the chilli, lemon zest and thyme and fry for a further 1 minute.

Drain the pasta, reserving 4 tablespoons of the cooking liquid, and return both to the pan. Stir in the hot garlic oil mixture, the lemon juice, the raw tuna, basil leaves, salt and pepper and a little extra olive oil. Serve at once.

350 g dried fusilli or other pasta

6 tablespoons extra virgin olive oil

4 garlic cloves, sliced

1–2 dried red chillies, deseeded and chopped

grated zest and juice of 1 unwaxed lemon

1 tablespoon chopped fresh thyme leaves

500 g tuna steak, chopped

a handful of fresh basil leaves

sea salt and freshly ground black pepper

serves 4

This sauce is best made as soon as the new season's tomatoes arrive in the shops, especially the vine-ripened varieties that we see more and more. If you don't have gas then simply plunge the tomatoes into boiling water for 1 minute, drain, refresh and peel the skin.

PASTA WITH FRESH TOMATO

Holding each tomato with tongs or a skewer, char them over a gas flame until the skins blister and start to shrivel. Peel off the skins, chop the flesh and put into a bowl. Add the oil, chillies, garlic, basil, sugar, salt and pepper and leave to infuse while you cook the pasta (or longer if possible).

Cook the pasta according to the instructions on the packet. Drain well and immediately stir in the fresh tomato sauce. Serve at once with the grated cheese.

1 kg ripe tomatoes

6 tablespoons extra virgin olive oil

2 red chillies, deseeded and chopped

2 garlic cloves, crushed

a bunch of fresh basil, chopped

1 teaspoon caster sugar

350 g dried spaghetti

cracked black pepper

grated Pecorino Sardo or Parmesan cheese, to serve

serves 4

Pasta is the archetypal fast food. This one is fast and fresh, with the ricotta melting into the hot pasta and coating it like a creamy sauce. The pine nuts give it crunch, while the herbs lend a fresh, scented flavour. If you don't have all the herbs listed here, use just rocket plus one other – the parsley or basil suggested, or perhaps chives, snipped with scissors.

PASTA WITH MELTED RICOTTA
AND HERBY PARMESAN SAUCE

Cook the pasta according to the instructions on the packet.

Meanwhile, heat the olive oil in a frying pan, add the pine nuts and fry gently until golden. Set aside.

Drain the cooked pasta, reserving 4 tablespoons of the cooking liquid, and return both to the pan. Add the pine nuts and their olive oil, the herbs, ricotta, half the Parmesan and plenty of cracked black pepper. Stir until evenly coated.

Serve in warmed bowls, with the remaining cheese sprinkled on top.

350 g dried penne or other pasta

6 tablespoons extra virgin olive oil

100 g pine nuts

125 g rocket leaves, chopped

2 tablespoons chopped fresh parsley

2 tablespoons chopped fresh basil

250 g fresh ricotta cheese, mashed

50 g freshly grated Parmesan cheese

sea salt and freshly ground black pepper

serves 4

SHRIMP FRIED RICE

Heat the oil in a wok and swirl to coat. Add the garlic, ginger and chilli and stir-fry for 30 seconds. Add the prawns, peas, spring onions and dried shrimp* and fry for 2 minutes until the prawns turn pink.

Using a spatula, push the mixture to one side, add the eggs and scramble until set. Then add the rice and stir over a high heat for 2 minutes until heated through.

Stir in the soy sauce, lemon juice and coriander and serve.

***Note** Packets of dried shrimp are available in Chinese or South-east Asian stores. They keep very well, even after opening.

2 tablespoons sunflower oil

2 garlic cloves, chopped

3 cm fresh ginger, peeled and grated

1 red chilli, deseeded and chopped

350 g small uncooked prawns, peeled, deveined and coarsely chopped

250 g frozen peas, thawed

6 spring onions, trimmed and sliced

4 tablespoons Asian dried shrimp*

2 eggs, lightly beaten

800 g cooked jasmine rice
(from 350 g uncooked rice)

3 tablespoons light soy sauce

freshly squeezed juice of ½ lemon

2 tablespoons chopped fresh coriander

serves 4

COCONUT AND LIME LEAF RICE

Put the rice into a sieve and wash under cold running water until the water runs clear. Drain and shake well.

Put the rice, coconut milk, lime leaves, lemongrass and salt into a heavy-based saucepan, add 350 ml water, bring to the boil, cover with a tight-fitting lid and simmer over very gentle heat for 20 minutes.

Remove the pan from the heat but leave undisturbed for a further 10 minutes. Fluff up with a fork and serve.

350 g jasmine rice

350 ml coconut milk

12 lime leaves, bashed

1 stalk of lemongrass, bruised

1 teaspoon salt

serves 6

Adding a nip of vodka right at the end adds a delightful flavour to this risotto. Although this recipe is slightly longer than most in the book, it is simple to make and always a terrific success with guests.

FENNEL AND LEMON RISOTTO

Soak the saffron in the hot stock until required. Finely chop the fennel and the fronds.

Melt half the butter in a frying pan, add the onion, chopped fennel, garlic and lemon zest and fry gently for 10 minutes until softened. Add the rice and stir for 30 seconds until the grains are glossy.

Meanwhile, heat the saffron stock to gentle simmer. Add a ladle of the stock to the rice and cook, stirring until absorbed. Continue adding the stock a little at a time, stirring, and cook for about 20 minutes until the liquid is absorbed and the rice is *al dente* (just done).

Remove the pan from the heat, stir in remaining butter, lemon juice, vodka, Parmesan, reserved fennel fronds, salt and pepper, cover, leave for 5 minutes, then serve.

a small pinch of saffron threads

1.25 litres hot Vegetable Stock (page 143)

1 large fennel bulb

125 g butter

1 onion, chopped

2 garlic cloves

juice and grated zest of 1 unwaxed lemon

300 g risotto rice

100 ml vodka

50 g freshly grated Parmesan cheese

sea salt and freshly ground black pepper

serves 4

PIZZA AND BREAD

By their very nature, pastry, pizza and bread doughs take time, but I did want to have some in the book. I love making them and there are many delicious breads that are relatively fast.

Making dough for pizzas is deceptive – although you should allow time for the dough to rise, the actual preparation and cooking time is short. I often make up a batch of dough, then go out to do the rest of the shopping. You can even leave it in a coolish place for the day, then knock it down just before baking. I have included three different pizza recipes and, if time is limited, you can use a package pizza dough mix or a frozen pizza base as an alternative.

The two bread recipes use dough that doesn't need to rise, drastically reducing the preparation time. The soda bread is a timeless classic, great served with soup. The cornbread is spiked with chilli and coriander. It is wonderfully savoury and can be eaten warm. Both are delicious toasted.

If you are really short of time you can cheat a little here and use a 500 g pack of frozen dough, cut in half — for two people you will need a whole packet. Follow the instructions on the pack but let rise for 15 minutes after you've rolled it out.

MOZZARELLA PIZZA
WITH GARLIC AND ROSEMARY

To make the dough, sift the flour into the bowl of a food mixer fitted with a dough hook attachment or a food processor fitted with a plastic blade. Add the yeast and salt, then work in the oil and water to form a soft dough.

Remove from the bowl and transfer to a floured work surface. Knead for 5 minutes until the dough is smooth, roll into a ball and put into an oiled bowl. Cover with clingfilm and let rise for about 45 minutes or until doubled in size.

Preheat the oven to its highest setting and put a pizza stone or baking sheet on the top shelf to heat.

Divide the risen dough in half and transfer one half to a well-floured surface. Roll it out to 30 cm diameter. Take the hot stone or baking sheet from the oven and carefully put the pizza base on top. Spread with half the mozzarella, garlic and rosemary leaves, then season with salt and pepper and sprinkle with a little extra oil. Bake in the preheated oven for 10–12 minutes until bubbling and lightly golden. Repeat with the second pizza.

It is best to eat the pizzas as soon as they come out of the oven, so I recommend sharing each one as they are cooked.

250 g strong white flour

1 teaspoon easy-blend dried yeast (half a 7 g sachet)

1 teaspoon salt

1 tablespoon extra virgin olive oil, plus extra to serve

125–150 ml hand-hot water

topping

250 g buffalo mozzarella, finely chopped

2 garlic cloves, sliced

2 sprigs of rosemary

sea salt and freshly ground black pepper

a pizza stone or baking sheet

serves 2–4

If you are making fresh pizza bases, I recommend that you cook the pizzas one at a time and eat them as soon as they are ready (unless you have two ovens). Use the conventional rather than fan setting on your oven to make sure you that have a good, crisp base on the pizza.

TOMATO PIZZA
WITH CAPERS AND ANCHOVIES

If using pizza base mix, prepare the dough according to the directions on the packet. Put the dough into a bowl and let rise until doubled in size.

Preheat the oven to its highest setting and put a pizza stone or baking sheet on the top shelf to heat.

Divide the risen dough in half and transfer one half to a well-floured surface. Roll it out to 30 cm diameter. Take the hot stone or baking sheet from the oven and carefully put the pizza base on top. Add half the tomatoes, capers, anchovies, mozzarella and a few basil leaves. Bake in the preheated oven for 10–12 minutes until bubbling and golden. Serve at once, then repeat to make a second pizza.

1 recipe Pizza Dough (page 107), 2 packets pizza base mix (about 200 g each), or 1 packet frozen pizza dough (500 g), halved

2 large ripe tomatoes, chopped

2 tablespoons capers, rinsed and drained

12 anchovy fillets in oil, drained and chopped

250 g buffalo mozzarella cheese, chopped

a few basil leaves

sea salt and freshly ground black pepper

a pizza stone or baking sheet

serves 2

Not a pizza, not a tart, but half-way between the two, and totally delicious. Usually, a pizza is cooked on a preheated pizza stone so that the base will be crisp. You can use a preheated baking sheet to achieve a good result.

MUSHROOM MASCARPONE PIZZA

If using pizza base mix, prepare the dough according to the directions on the packet. Put the pizza dough into a bowl and let rise until doubled in size.

Preheat the oven to its highest setting and put a pizza stone or baking sheet on the top shelf to heat.

Heat the oil in a frying pan and fry the garlic and thyme for 1 minute. Add the mushrooms and fry for a further 4–5 minutes until they are brown but haven't started to release their juices. Season with salt and pepper.

Divide the risen dough in half and transfer one half to a well-floured surface. Roll it out to 30 cm diameter. Take the hot pizza stone or baking sheet from the oven and carefully put the pizza base on top. Spoon half the mushrooms on top and dot with half the mascarpone.

Sprinkle with half the Parmesan and bake in the preheated oven for 10–12 minutes until bubbling and golden. Serve at once and then repeat to make a second pizza.

1 recipe Pizza Dough (page 107), 2 packets pizza base mix (about 200 g each), or 1 packet frozen pizza dough (500 g), halved

6 tablespoons extra virgin olive oil

2 garlic cloves, sliced

1 tablespoon chopped fresh thyme leaves

500 g small open mushrooms, sliced

200 g mascarpone cheese

25 g freshly grated Parmesan cheese

sea salt and freshly ground black pepper

a pizza stone or baking sheet

serves 2–4

This is the classic Irish soda bread made with bicarbonate of soda as the raising agent rather than yeast. This means that the dough can be baked immediately, rather than having to let it rise as with a yeasted dough. Quick and easy to make.

SODA BREAD

Put the flour, bicarbonate of soda, salt and sugar into a bowl and mix well. Make a well in the centre, add the buttermilk and gradually work it into the flour to make a soft dough.

Knead on a lightly floured surface for 5 minutes and then shape into a flattened round loaf. Transfer to an oiled baking sheet and, using a sharp knife, cut a cross in the top of the dough. Sprinkle with a little extra flour.

Bake in a preheated oven 230°C (450°F) Gas 8 for 15 minutes, then reduce the heat to 200°C (400°F) Gas 6 and bake for a further 30 minutes until risen and the loaf sounds hollow when tapped underneath.

Transfer to a wire rack and let cool completely.

400 g plain wholemeal flour, plus extra for sprinkling

1 teaspoon bicarbonate of soda

1 teaspoon salt

1 teaspoon sugar

300 ml buttermilk

a baking sheet, oiled

makes 1 small loaf

I like to cook this cornbread in a deep loaf tin so that later it can be sliced and toasted more easily. However, if you are short of time, pour the mixture into a greased and base-lined baking tin and cook for 20–25 minutes.

CHILLI CORNBREAD

Sift the flour and baking powder into a bowl and stir in the cornmeal and salt.

Mix the eggs, buttermilk and oil in a second bowl, then, using a wooden spoon, stir into the dry ingredients to make a smooth batter. Stir in the corn, chilli and coriander and pour into the prepared loaf tin.

Bake in a preheated oven at 200°C (400°F) Gas 6 for 40 minutes. Let cool in the tin for 5 minutes, then remove from the tin and let cool on a wire rack.

75 g plain flour

1 tablespoon baking powder

200 g medium cornmeal or polenta

1 teaspoon salt

3 eggs, beaten

300 ml buttermilk

4 tablespoons extra virgin olive oil

200 g canned sweetcorn kernels, drained

1–2 red chillies, deseeded and chopped

2 tablespoons chopped fresh coriander

a deep loaf tin, 1 kg, greased and base-lined

serves 8–12

When I was a child, every main meal ended with a pudding, but today this seems to be something most of us reserve for a dinner party or at best the weekends. Time and health issues may well be the reason, but not all sweet things have to be rich and heavy, and some don't take long to prepare. Good-quality fresh fruit needs little to adorn it – just pick flavours that work well together and combine them simply.

If your sweet tooth is utterly incorrigible, you will probably decide that chocolate is worth whatever time it takes, so of course I have included some drinks and puddings for you. Other 'proper puddings' take a little more time, but they're worth every second, I'm sure you would agree.

Fast & Fresh wouldn't be complete without a section on drinks, and although many drinks are already quick and simple to prepare (only a few seconds to open that chilled bottle of wine), I'm always on the lookout for new combinations – James Bondi is one of my favourites, now that I live in Sydney.

PUDDINGSANDDRINKS

Strawberries and black pepper are surprisingly good partners. The orange flower water adds a lovely perfumed quality to the strawberries, but can be omitted.

STRAWBERRIES WITH BLACK PEPPER

Hull the strawberries and cut in half. Sprinkle with the orange flower water, if using, and with the sugar and black pepper. Chill for 15 minutes and serve.

Note Strawberries should be washed and dried before hulling, not after, otherwise they fill up with water.

500 g strawberries

1 tablespoon orange flower water (optional)

1 tablespoon caster sugar

2 teaspoons cracked black pepper

serves 4

Rosewater, like orange flower water, is sold in the baking section of supermarkets, in chemist shops, and in ethnic food stores specializing in Middle Eastern or Indian products.

RHUBARB COMPOTE WITH YOGURT

Cut the rhubarb into 5 cm slices and put into a saucepan. Add the caster sugar and 4 tablespoons water. Bring to the boil, cover and simmer gently for 15 minutes until the rhubarb has softened. Taste and stir in a little extra sugar if necessary. Transfer to a dish and let cool.

Put the yoghurt, honey and rosewater into a bowl, mix well, then serve with the rhubarb.

500 g rhubarb, trimmed

50 g caster sugar, or to taste

125 g plain yoghurt

1 tablespoon clear honey

$1/2$ tablespoon rosewater

serves 4

Vanilla sugar is easy to make – just put a couple of vanilla pods in a jar of sugar and leave them there, topping up with fresh sugar as necessary. You can use the pods for cooking, pat dry with kitchen paper, then return them to the sugar.

ROASTED MASCARPONE PEACHES

Cut the peaches in half, remove the stones and arrange the fruit cut side up in a roasting tin. Pour over the honey and bake in a preheated oven at 200°C (400°F) Gas 6 for about 20 minutes until softened and lightly golden.

Mix the mascarpone with the vanilla sugar and lemon juice and spoon onto the hot peaches. Serve at once.

4 large ripe peaches

2 tablespoons clear honey

150 g mascarpone cheese

3 tablespoons vanilla sugar

1 tablespoon freshly squeezed lemon juice

serves 4

Melon and ginger are a classic combination of flavours and this simple version is perfect for a warm summer's day. You can use any type of melon, but my favourite is cantaloupe.

MELON WITH GINGER SYRUP

Put the sugar and 150 ml water into a small saucepan and heat gently to dissolve the sugar. Bring to the boil, add the ginger and lemon juice and simmer gently for 3 minutes. Remove from the heat and let cool.

Cut the melon into wedges, scoop out the seeds and serve sprinkled with ginger syrup.

75 g caster sugar

2.5 cm fresh ginger, peeled and finely chopped

freshly squeezed juice of ½ large lemon

1 large ripe melon

serves 4–6

Fruit fritters are delicious and very simple to make. I serve them with cinnamon ice cream, available in some supermarkets and specialist food stores. Cinnamon and banana make an excellent flavour combination, but choose your own favourite flavour.

BANANA FRITTERS
WITH CINNAMON ICE CREAM

Peel the bananas, cut into 4 chunks, then cut the chunks in half lengthways.

To make the batter, sift the flour and salt into a bowl, beat in the egg yolk, ginger beer or sparkling water and oil to form a smooth batter. Whisk the egg white in a separate bowl until soft peaks form, then fold into the batter.

Heat 5 cm sunflower oil in deep saucepan until it reaches 180°C (350°F) or until a cube of bread turns golden brown in 30 seconds.

Dip the banana chunks into the batter and deep-fry in batches of 3–4 for about 1 minute until the batter is crisp and golden. Drain on kitchen paper and keep them warm in a moderate oven while you cook the remainder. Serve with a scoop of cinnamon ice cream.

2 large bananas

cinnamon ice cream, to serve

ginger batter

40 g plain flour

a pinch of salt

1 egg, separated

75 ml ginger beer or sparkling water

1 tablespoon sunflower oil, plus extra for deep-frying

serves 4

Bread and butter pudding was one of my childhood favourites, and I couldn't have been happier than when it enjoyed a revival a couple of years ago. This is my version of this wonderful retro recipe, and if you make them in individual dishes, they will cook in under 20 minutes.

BREAD AND BUTTER PUDDINGS

Put the milk, cream, vanilla essence and 3 tablespoons of the sugar into a saucepan and heat until the sugar dissolves.

Put the eggs into a bowl, whisk well, stir in 2–3 tablespoons of the hot milk mixture to warm the eggs, then stir in the remainder of the hot milk.

Lightly toast the tea cakes or hot cross buns and cut into quarters. Divide between the 6 prepared ramekins and sprinkle with the sultanas.

Pour in the custard, grate a little nutmeg over the top, then sprinkle with the remaining sugar. Bake in a preheated oven at 180°C (350°F) Gas 4 for 18–20 minutes until firm. Let cool a little, then serve warm.

300 ml milk

300 ml double cream

$\frac{1}{2}$ teaspoon vanilla essence

4 tablespoons caster sugar

3 eggs

6 tea cakes or hot cross buns, halved

50 g sultanas

1 whole nutmeg

6 ramekins, 200 ml each, well buttered

serves 6

Even if you never make puddings at any other time, you probably do when you have people to dinner. Perfect for such an occasion, these little plum fudge puddings can be prepared well in advance, then cooked just before serving.

PLUM FUDGE PUDDINGS

Put the butter, honey and cream into a saucepan and heat until melted. Put the sugar, spice and breadcrumbs into a bowl and stir well.

Divide half the buttery fudge mixture between the ramekin dishes and top with a layer of plum slices and half the breadcrumb mix. Add the remaining plums and breadcrumbs, then spoon over the remaining sauce.

Set on a baking sheet and bake in a preheated oven at 200°C (400°F) Gas 6 for 20 minutes. Remove from the oven and let cool for 5 minutes, then carefully unmould the puddings and serve with a spoonful of crème fraîche.

50 g unsalted butter

50 g honey

2 tablespoons double cream

2 tablespoons soft brown sugar

1 teaspoon ground mixed spice

75 g fresh white breadcrumbs

2 ripe plums, halved, stoned and thinly sliced

crème fraîche, to serve

4 ramekins, 150 ml each

serves 4

Chocolate and rosemary may sound an unusual combination but in fact the flavours go very well together. Remove the mousses from the refrigerator about 1 hour before serving so that they can return to room temperature.

CHOCOLATE AND ROSEMARY POTS

Put the cream and rosemary sprigs into a saucepan and heat slowly just to boiling point. Remove from the heat and leave to infuse for 20 minutes.

Strain into a clean pan, add the chocolate and heat very gently until the chocolate melts (don't let the mixture boil). Remove from the heat, let cool slightly, then stir in the egg yolks one at a time. Finally add the butter, stirring until melted.

Pour the mixture into the espresso cups and let cool. Chill for 2 hours. Spear each chocolate pot with a rosemary sprig, if using, just before serving.

300 ml single cream

2 sprigs of rosemary, bruised, plus 6 extra, to serve (optional)

200 g plain chocolate, chopped

2 egg yolks

25 g unsalted butter

6 espresso cups or small ramekins

serves 6

Brownies are everyone's favourite chocolate indulgence. They're not complicated to make, but the better the chocolate, the better they will be. The most important rule is to aim for the right texture – just set on top, but wonderfully gooey and melting on the inside. Most people can't resist eating them the minute they come out of the oven – plain or with a cup of coffee. But if you can wait, try them as a quick pudding, with cream or ice cream.

CHOCOLATE AND CINNAMON BROWNIES

Put the hazelnuts into a dry frying pan and toast over medium heat until aromatic. Do not let burn. Let cool, then chop coarsely.

Put the chocolate and butter into a heatproof bowl set over a saucepan of simmering water and melt gently. Put the eggs and sugar into a bowl and beat until pale. Stir in the melted chocolate, flour, cinnamon, white chocolate chips and chopped hazelnuts.

Spoon into the prepared tin and bake in a preheated oven at 190°C (375°F) Gas 5 for about 35–40 minutes until the top sets but the mixture still feels soft underneath.

Remove from the oven and let cool in the tin. Serve cut into squares.

75 g hazelnuts

275 g dark chocolate with at least 70 per cent cocoa solids

225 g unsalted butter

3 eggs

225 g caster sugar

75 g self-raising flour

2 teaspoons ground cinnamon

100 g white chocolate chips

a baking tin, 18 x 28 cm, greased and base-lined

serves 8–12

These pastry puffs filled with chocolate remind me of the delicious French pastry, *pain au chocolat*. Making them with frozen puff pastry is even faster than a trip to the pâtisserie. If you prefer, you can use plain dark chocolate instead of the white.

SPICED WHITE CHOCOLATE PUFFS

Put the pastry on a floured work surface and cut each sheet into 4 pieces, 10 cm square.

Put 3 pieces of chocolate onto each square, then add a light dusting of mixed spice (I use a small tea strainer). Dampen the edges with a little water, then fold them over diagonally to form a triangle. Press the edges together to seal, then, using the blade of a sharp knife, gently tap the sealed edges several times (this will help the pastry rise).

Transfer the triangles to the baking sheet. Put the egg yolk and milk into a small bowl, beat well, then brush over the pastry. Bake in a preheated oven at 220°C (425°F) Gas 7 for 10–15 minutes until risen and golden.

Remove from the oven, let cool for 5 minutes, lightly dust with cocoa powder and serve with coffee.

2 sheets ready-rolled puff pastry, thawed if frozen

plain flour, for dusting

175 g white chocolate, cut into 24 squares

ground mixed spice

1 egg yolk

2 tablespoons milk

cocoa powder, to serve

a baking sheet, greased

makes 8

The perfect nightcap, sleepytime chocolate with a hint of romantic after-dinner mints – just the thing to send you off into a peaceful sleep, or warm you up on a chilly winter's afternoon.

MINTED HOT CHOCOLATE

Put the milk and mint sprigs into a saucepan and heat very gently until boiling. Boil for 1 minute, then remove from the heat. Discard the mint.

Divide the chocolate between 2 mugs. Stir in the milk and continue to stir until melted. Serve the sugar separately, if using.

600 ml milk

4 sprigs fresh mint, bruised lightly to extract flavour

50 g plain chocolate, chopped

sugar, to taste (optional)

serves 2

Kids will love this shake, particularly with a spoonful of extra ice cream. I've made it optional, but of course it can't possibly be!

CHOCOLATE AND BANANA CINNAMON SHAKE

Peel and chop the bananas. Put the ice cream, bananas, milk and cinnamon into a blender and purée until smooth. Pour into tall glasses and serve with an extra scoop of chocolate ice cream, if using.

2 bananas

4 scoops chocolate ice cream, plus extra to serve (optional)

300 ml milk

1 teaspoon ground cinnamon

serves 4

Tisane is the French word for an infusion of herbs, flowers or other aromatics. I think it's a beautiful word for this deliciously spicy drink, which I've chilled down to make a great contrast between hot and cold.

CHILLED LEMONGRASS TISANE

Put the chilli into a heatproof jug with the lemongrass, ginger and sugar, then add 1 litre boiling water and the lemon juice and stir to dissolve the sugar. Leave to infuse until cold.

Strain the cooled liquid and chill for at least 30 minutes. Serve in tall glasses with mint leaves and ice cubes.

1–2 red chillies, deseeded and sliced

2–4 stalks of lemongrass, outer leaves discarded, inner section finely sliced

5 cm fresh ginger, peeled and sliced

50 g caster sugar

freshly squeezed juice of 2 lemons

mint leaves and ice cubes, to serve

serves 4

My juicer has a citrus attachment as well as a juicer, so this drink couldn't be simpler. If you don't have the citrus press, just peel the oranges and put them through the regular juicer (don't forget to remove all the bitter white pith).

ORANGE AND APPLE REFRESHER

Push the oranges, apples and the ginger through the juicer. Half-fill 2 tall glasses with ice cubes, pour the juice over the top and serve.

2 large oranges, peeled

2 Granny Smith apples

3 cm fresh ginger, peeled

ice cubes, to serve

a juicing machine

serves 2

JAMES BONDI

A variation on the classic champagne cocktail I found at a funky Sydney bar, beside the famous beach that inspired the pun.

Put the sugar lumps into 6 champagne flutes, add the vodka and stir with a spoon until the sugar completely dissolves (crush it slightly if necessary).

Add a dash of bitters to each one, top up with champagne and serve.

6 brown sugar lumps

60 ml vodka

a dash of Angostura bitters

1 bottle chilled champagne

serves 6

CAMPARI GRAPEFRUIT SLUSH

600 ml ice cubes

100 ml Campari

200 ml sweetened ruby grapefruit juice

serves 4

Campari and grapefruit juice are a marriage made in heaven, lovely with or without sugar.

Put the ice cubes into a blender and grind until crushed. Add the Campari and grapefruit juice and blend until slushy. Serve in chilled glasses with short cocktail straws.

PEACH SANGRIA

A white wine variation of the more classic Spanish aperitif, cool and delightful on a hot summer's day.

Pour the wine into a large jug, add the peach liqueur, sliced peaches, orange and lemon. Add ice cubes and stir well. When ready to serve, half-fill tall glasses with ice cubes, wine and fruit, then top up with the lemonade.

1 bottle chilled dry white wine

4 tablespoons peach liqueur

4 large ripe peaches, sliced

1 orange, sliced

1 unwaxed lemon, sliced

ice cubes

chilled lemonade

serves 6

THE BASICS: FLAVOURED OILS, BUTTERS AND DRESSINGS

OILS Herbs, spices and aromatics can all be added to oils to enhance the flavour and provide another valuable staple to the kitchen cupboard. They should be infused in the oil for about 7 days for the best results. Heating the oil and flavourings over a gentle heat speeds up the process as well as killing off any harmful bacteria. It is always best to strain the oil after the flavours have developed, then store in a cool place.

Another method of flavouring oil is to purée the herb and oil, then strain off the residue. This gives a vibrant green oil with a lovely flavour. As well as recipes for Fragrant Garlic Oil (page 21), Basil Oil (page 26), here are:

Thyme Oil

6 sprigs fresh thyme

600 ml extra virgin olive oil

makes 600 ml

Crush the thyme sprigs lightly with a rolling pin to help release the aroma. Put them into a screw-top jar. Add the oil and leave to infuse for 7 days. Strain into a clean jar before using.

Chilli Oil

300 ml extra virgin olive oil

4 dried red chillies, coarsely chopped

makes 300 ml

Put the oil and chillies into a screw-top jar and leave to infuse for 2 days before using.

BUTTERS Flavouring butter with spices and herbs is great fun as well as cost effective – just think of the amount of herbs you throw away when you have chopped up a few too many. There are so many different combinations of flavours you can use. Try Horseradish and Chive (page 80), or one of the following:

Mustard and Tarragon Butter

2 tablespoons chopped fresh tarragon

1 tablespoon wholegrain mustard

125 g softened butter

makes 125 g

Finely chop the tarragon leaves and beat into the butter with the mustard. Roll, wrap and freeze.

Coriander, Lime and Pepper Butter

2 tablespoons chopped fresh coriander

125 g softened butter

grated zest and juice of 1 unwaxed lime

1/2 teaspoon cracked black pepper

makes 125 g

Finely chop the coriander leaves and then beat into the butter with the remaining ingredients. Roll into a small log, wrap in clingfilm and freeze until required.

Mint and Cumin Butter

Although this is a great partner for lamb chops, I also like it tossed with cooked baby new potatoes and left for a few minutes to infuse.

1/2 tablespoon cumin seeds

2 tablespoons chopped fresh mint

125 g softened butter

makes 125 g

Dry-fry the cumin seeds in a frying pan for about 3 minutes until they start to 'pop'. Cool and then crush with a mortar and pestle.

Finely chop the mint leaves and beat into the butter with the cumin seeds. Wrap, roll and freeze as above.

DRESSINGS I always like to keep a jar of homemade dressing in the refrigerator so that making a salad for lunch takes just a few minutes. If the dressing includes herbs, it is best made just before you use it – or make up the dressing, but leave the herbs until the last minute. You'll find other dressing recipes throughout the book – Lemon and Coriander (page 55), Black Bean (page 31) and others – but here are some of my favourites:

Classic French Dressing

150 ml extra virgin olive oil

2 tablespoons white wine vinegar

2 teaspoons Dijon mustard

½ teaspoon sugar

sea salt and freshly ground black pepper

makes 175 ml

Put all the ingredients into screw-top jar, shake until amalgamated. Store in the refrigerator and shake again before using.

Salmoriglio

An Italian dressing served with grilled fish or chicken – I love it with red mullet or bream. Look out for the sweet Italian-style lemons now more widely available.

200 ml extra virgin olive oil

freshly squeezed juice of 1 large lemon

2 tablespoons chopped fresh parsley

2 garlic cloves, crushed

a pinch of dried oregano

sea salt and freshly ground black pepper

makes 225 ml

Put all the ingredients into a screw-top jar and shake well. Serve the same day.

Reduced Balsamic Vinegar

Reducing a cheap balsamic vinegar produces a sauce almost as good as an aged balsamic, which would cost a great deal more. It may seem like a terrible waste simply to boil away the vinegar but the resulting thick glaze can be used sparingly and will provide a delicious finish to many dishes.

300 ml balsamic vinegar

makes 100 ml

Put the vinegar into a small saucepan and boil gently until reduced by two-thirds and reaches the consistency of a thick syrup. Let cool and then store in a clean jar.

SAUCES AND STOCKS

SAUCES Many useful sauces appear in this book. Try Wasabi Mayonnaise (page 14) or Pistachio and Mint Pesto (page 50). Other favourites include:

Mayonnaise

For a gentler sauce, I use a milder oil such as French or Spanish, or a mixture of extra virgin and pure olive oils.

2 egg yolks

2 teaspoons white wine vinegar or lemon juice

1/4 teaspoon salt

2 teaspoons Dijon mustard

300 ml extra virgin olive oil

freshly ground black pepper

makes about 300 ml

Put the egg yolks, vinegar, salt and mustard into a food processor and blend until frothy. With the machine running, slowly pour in the oil until the sauce is thick and glossy. You may have to thin it slightly by blending in 1–2 tablespoons boiling water. Season to taste. Cover the surface with clingfilm and store in the refrigerator for up to 5 days.

Quick Tomato Sauce

This quick, delicious sauce can be tossed through pasta for a simple supper dish, spread over a pizza base or used as the base for bean dishes or main courses.

800 g canned chopped tomatoes

4 garlic cloves, crushed

4 tablespoons extra virgin olive oil

1 teaspoon caster sugar

1 teaspoon dried oregano

2 tablespoons chopped fresh basil

sea salt and freshly ground black pepper

serves 4–6

Put the tomatoes, garlic, oil, sugar, oregano, salt and pepper into a saucepan, bring to the boil and simmer, covered, over gentle heat for 30 minutes until reduced and tasty.

Stir in the basil and adjust seasonings. Serve as required or cool and refrigerate overnight.

Quick Romesco Sauce

50 g blanched almonds

3 garlic cloves, chopped

75 ml extra virgin olive oil

2 ripe tomatoes, coarsely chopped

2 tablespoons red wine vinegar

2 teaspoons smoked paprika

1 teaspoon caster sugar

1/4–1 teaspoon chilli powder

sea salt

makes 300 ml

Put the almonds into a dry frying pan and fry over medium heat until browned. Cool, then transfer to a food processor, add the garlic and blend briefly until coarsely ground.

Add the remaining ingredients, purée until fairly smooth, then season to taste. Store in the refrigerator for up to 3 days.

Almond and Parsley Pesto

This version of pesto can be tossed through pasta, served with chicken or used as a dip.

50 g blanched almonds

25 g pine nuts

a large bunch of flat leaf parsley

2 garlic cloves, chopped

175 ml extra virgin olive oil

2 tablespoons grated Parmesan

sea salt and freshly ground black pepper

makes about 300 ml

Put the almonds into a dry pan and fry over medium heat until browned, transfer to a bowl. Repeat with the pine nuts and let cool.

Put the nuts into a food processor, add the parsley and garlic and blend briefly until coarsely ground. Add the oil and purée until smooth and vibrantly green. Stir in the cheese and season to taste. Store in the refrigerator for up to 5 days.

STOCKS Though recipes in this book are designed to be fast and fresh, I include these three basic stocks – make them up when you have time and freeze them for later. You can buy fresh stocks, but if you use stock cubes, try to find some with the organic label.

Vegetable Stock

2 onions, chopped

2 potatoes, chopped

2 leeks, sliced

4 carrots, sliced

1 large celery stalk, sliced

4 tomatoes, chopped

150 g mushrooms, chopped

4 garlic cloves, chopped

50 g rice or green lentils

150 ml dry white wine

4 sprigs of parsley

2 sprigs of thyme

2 teaspoons sea salt

1 teaspoon black pepper

makes about 1.5 litres

Put all the ingredients into a saucepan and add 1.75 litres water. Bring to the boil, cover and simmer for 1 hour.

Strain through a fine sieve and taste. Either reduce the stock by simmering gently to enhance the flavour, or cool and refrigerate for up to 3 days or freeze for up to 3 months.

Chicken Stock

1 kg chicken

2 carrots, coarsely chopped

3 celery stalks, coarsely chopped

1 onion, chopped

1 leek, chopped

6 garlic cloves, chopped

2 tomatoes, chopped

2 fresh bay leaves

2 sprigs fresh thyme

6 white peppercorns

1 teaspoon salt

makes about 1.5 litres

Put all the ingredients into a saucepan and and water to cover, about 2 litres. Bring to the boil, skim off the foam and simmer gently, uncovered, for 1 hour.

Strain through a fine sieve and let cool completely. Refrigerate until required or freeze for up to 3 months.

Fish Stock

1 kg fish trimmings

900 ml dry white wine

900 ml water

2 carrots, coarsely chopped

2 celery stalks, coarsely chopped

1 onion, chopped

1 leek, sliced

1 garlic clove, chopped

2 fresh bay leaves

2 sprigs of parsley

6 white peppercorns

1 teaspoon salt

makes about 900 ml

Wash the fish trimmings and put into a large saucepan with all the remaining ingredients. Bring to the boil, skim off the foam and simmer gently for 30 minutes.

Strain into a clean pan and simmer until the stock is reduced to about 900 ml. Let cool completely and refrigerate until required or freeze for up to 3 months.

INDEX